LORD OF THE FORTY DAYS

Lord of the Forty Days

MEDITATIONS FOR LENT

FRANK TOPPING

DIMENSIONS
FOR LIVING
NASHVILLE

LORD OF THE FORTY DAYS:
MEDITATIONS FOR LENT

Copyright © Frank Topping 1983

*Dimensions for Living edition published 2003 by arrangement
with The Lutterworth Press*

All rights reserved.
No part of this work may be reproduced or transmitted in any form or by any means, electronic or mechanical, including photocopying and recording, or by any information storage or retrieval system, except as may be expressly permitted by the 1976 Copyright Act or in writing from the publisher. Requests for permission should be addressed to Dimensions for Living, P.O. Box 801, 201 Eighth Avenue South, Nashville, TN 37202-0801.

This book is printed on recycled, acid-free, elemental-chlorine–free paper.

ISBN 0-687-07549-1

Scripture quotations are from the Revised Standard Version of the Bible copyright © 1946, 1952, 1971, 1973 by the Division of Christian Education of the National Council of the Churches of Christ in the USA, with those for meditations 8, 10, 16, 25, 27, 28, and 33 adapted.

The Graeca® font used to print this work is available from Linguist's Software, Inc., PO Box 580, Edmonds, WA 98020-0580 tel (206) 775-1130.

To Derrick and Nancy Greeves,
who in the early days fed mind and body

CONTENTS

Preface 9
1. Not by Bread Alone? 13
2. The Poor in Spirit 15
3. Those Who Mourn 18
4. The Meek 20
5. Righteousness 23
6. The Merciful 25
7. The Pure in Heart 27
8. The Peacemakers 29
9. Theirs Is the Kingdom 31
10. Let the Light Shine 33
11. Love Your Enemies 35
12. Our Father 38
13. Our Daily Bread 40
14. Forgive Us 42
15. Testing 44
16. Trials 46
17. Treasure 48

18. Anxiety 50
19. Judging 52
20. Solid Rock 54
21. I Am Not Worthy 56
22. Why Are You Afraid? 58
23. Healing 60
24. Speaking Out 62
25. Real Life 64
26. Rest 66
27. Whited Sepulchres 68
28. Who Do You Say That I Am? 70
29. Like Children 72
30. Seventy Times Seven 74
31. The Resurrection of the Dead 76
32. The Great Commandment 78
33. The Least of These 80
34. Take, Eat 82
35. Before the Cock Crows 84
36. Take This Cup 86
37. The Spirit Is Willing 88
38. Love Is Crucified 90
39. To the End of the World 92
40. Peace 94

PREFACE

This book can only be a starting point, for it is impossible to write down a meditation; we cannot yet photograph thoughts and unspoken prayer.

To *meditate* is to "plan" or "consider mentally," and so, for the reader, the notes that accompany the New Testament texts will not be the meditation; the meditation will be the thoughts that follow. These notes were made during and after meditation and are not meant to be read one after the other but alongside the complete biblical passage from which each text is taken, together with a modern commentary.

Let me give you an example of how I explore a particular text. The Sermon on the Mount begins with the Beatitudes, a lyrical series of blessings. First I look at the background or setting of the sermon, because *where* Jesus is speaking and to *whom* do have a bearing on the meaning of what he is saying. We have to play detective and follow every clue. For example, the Sermon on the *Mount* in Matthew's Gospel becomes the Sermon on the *Plain* in Luke's Gospel. In Matthew, Jesus goes up the mountain to escape the crowds. In Luke, he comes down to a level place to speak to the crowd. I suppose we could come to a compromise about *where* Jesus spoke, as he might have been neither up nor down, but halfway. There is, in fact, a level area halfway down the hill behind the ruins of Capernaum.

To *whom* he is speaking is a far more important question though. In Matthew, Jesus sits down with his *disciples* and teaches them. And in Luke, surrounded by crowds, he looks directly at his *disciples*. Luke makes a point of this when he says, "And he lifted up his eyes on his *disciples*." Jesus is speaking to a very special group at this particular moment, the ones whom he had chosen, called. Knowing this helps us understand the significance of the first beatitude:

"Blessed are the poor in spirit, for theirs is the kingdom of heaven."

Now the detective work takes another turn. The English word *poor* does not mean poor as we understand it but is a translation of the Greek word πτωχονζ (*ptockos*). This was, in turn, the translation of an Aramaic word used to describe a Hebrew concept of the *ani* or *anaw,* which meant "the humble," "the pious," "those close to God," or "those who seek God." When Jews, in their religious teachings, used the word *ani,* they meant not the destitute but the pious who sought God. So the first beatitude takes on a different meaning and could read:

"Blessed are *those who seek God* in spirit."

Now let us look at *in spirit*. Luke does not use it at all, and Matthew has τνευμστιγοω (*pneumatikos*), which means literally "belonging to the wind" or "freely" or "in spirit" or "willingly." So the whole verse could say:

"Blessed are those who seek God—willingly, freely."

Jesus is saying this directly to his disciples who have given up everything to follow him:

"Blessed are you who have willingly put yourselves in the path of the wind of God."

Having delved into the meaning of the words as they were used in Jesus' day, then I ask myself what they mean to me in my day. When I have done all this, I then lay my study and thought before God in prayer.

I am a dreadful book vandal. If the book is mine, I am

inclined to scribble in the margins. Looking at the scribbling on my original manuscript, I see that I have used a number of books to help me in my study. I also find it helpful to look at the passage in several different translations of the Bible.

Here then are the notes made during and after a personal meditational study of the words of Christ. Because they are personal, they are inevitably inadequate. Do not hesitate to pencil your own notes in the margins. Then each meditation will become your own.

Frank Topping

1. NOT BY BREAD ALONE?
(Matthew 4:4)

Man shall not live by bread alone.

And yet, most of us live by little else.
By the sweat of our brows
we toil for bread,
pray for our daily bread.
This very day,
the hungry will sit and wait
for crumbs from the rich man's table.
Many will not survive the day.
To the hungry,
there is only one kind of bread.

From childhood I was taught,
trained, prepared for the day
when I would earn my bread;
learned from my betters
that the stuff of life
was security,
bread on the table
and a pension.

I have never starved;
I have been very hungry.
I have lived on rationed food, hardtack;
I have lived in a dry land where water is precious;
I have longed for days of plenty.
Yet when they came,
those milk and honey days
when thirst was quenched
and belly filled
and pockets jingled,
still, there was an aching void,
an empty shell that echoed to the whisper,
"Man shall not live by bread alone."

With bread enough
I might survive
a decent span of years.
But merely to survive
is not enough,
does not draw near the promise
that stirred within that snatched first breath
that gave me life.

Breath of God,
feed me with the bread of life
that was broken for me.
Let me be nurtured
by the compassion of Christ,
strengthened
by the forgiveness of Christ,
built up
in the hope of Christ,
that I might grow
in the love of Christ
and reach toward the measure of the stature
of the fullness of Christ.

2. THE POOR IN SPIRIT
(Matthew 5:3)

Blessed are the poor in spirit.

What living things
are words and language!
How frequently they change
their shades of meaning.
In Hebrew, Aramaic, or Greek,
what complexity lies in these few words,
"Blessed are the poor in spirit."

Poor,
an English translation
of a Greek translation
of a Hebrew concept
that did not mean *destitute* or *impoverished*
but referred to *the righteous remnant,*
the *faithful few*, the *pious,*
the *humble who seek God.*

In spirit
attempts to encapsulate
the life of a phrase that meant

belonging to the wind,
freely, willingly.

So did Jesus say,
in his marketplace tongue,
"Blessed are
the humble who seek God *willingly*"?
And does he say it still, to me,
even as I choose
to turn my face away?

Blessed are those
who seek God willingly;
blessed indeed
to have such courage.
There is a reluctance in my search,
a fear of finding,
a deep-rooted fear of the consequences.
I hardly dare lift my head
lest I should meet the gaze
of love so holy, so other,
so different from mine
that the things I cherish might
be seen as dust
and dross
and vanity
before those eyes.

Blessed are those
who seek God, willingly.
Lord,
out of the depths of unwillingness,
out of the stupor of weakness

and self-interest,
hear my cry.

Lord,
if I cannot willingly
seek you,
then will you,
in your mercy, lovingly
seek me.

3. THOSE WHO MOURN
(Matthew 5:4)

(Thinking about this text, I wrote a song that was set to music by Donald Swann. The song was broadcast on radio and television, I have included it here because so many people have asked for the words. On one occasion, I was stopped on a railway station by a complete stranger, who quoted the last four lines of the first verse from memory. For this particular person, the words summed up feelings experienced when a lifetime partner had died.)

Blessed are those who mourn,
for they shall be comforted.

As signposts pointing separate ways
for lover, husband, wife,
farewells and partings cleave my days,
make chapters in my life.
Yet those I love take part of me
with them when they leave,
and close within the heart of me
is locked the love I grieve.

Without love, to mourn is madness.
Without love, why weep?
Without love there is no sadness,
no grief, no fitful sleep.
Only love can mourn,
love that laughed and cried,
love well-used and worn,
love that never died.

Love blesses the bereaved,
love prepares the way,
love is not deceived
when death has had his say.
Love in Christ puts death to flight,
love prepares the place
where love, with love, will all unite
before that loving face.

4. THE MEEK
(Matthew 5:5)

Blessed are the meek,
for they shall inherit the earth.

Meekness!
Dear God, the very word
sticks in my throat.
My every instinct is hostile
to the thought of submission.
Ask me to yield,
and resistance stiffens.
Meekness embraces surrender,
and complete surrender to your will
is my stumbling block.

How emptily have I offered
to live to your glory
while clinging to my need for applause.
How falsely have I laid my gifts
before your throne
while the core of me
continued to claim them for myself.
In spite of my grim resistance

I know that there is strength
in gentleness;
there is resilience
in humility.

Lord,
teach me to accept
that when wickedness nailed goodness
to the cross,
it was evil that received
the mortal blow;
that in gentleness and love
is strength that never fails;
that it is the proud who fall
and the meek who inherit the earth.

Lord,
forgive me
for the misuse of my gifts.
Forgive me
my boasting, my arrogance, my pride.
Teach me to use my talents
not merely for self-satisfaction
but in the cause of love.

Give me the strength to be gentle.
Give me the lion-heart
that is humble.
Give me the wisdom
to see my faults—
and the courage to admit them.
Give me patience
to understand an opposing view.

Teach me tolerance.
Teach me
to yield, to submit,
to surrender
to your will.
Teach me the meekness
which inherits the earth.

5. RIGHTEOUSNESS
(Matthew 5:6)

Blessed are those who hunger and thirst
for righteousness,
for they shall be satisfied.

Lord,
my hunger is rarely
for goodness, truth, and love.
I have a natural leaning
toward selfishness and sin.
My daily diet includes
liberal helpings of salacious tales,
hot from the press.

I drink in stories of dishonesty,
violence, and hatred;
grow fat on self-indulgent gossip;
and cynicism is savored
as a substitute for wisdom.

Lord,
I wish I could be righteous
in the truest sense,

not self-righteous
but a lover of virtue and justice,
bound by the law of love,
loving God
and my neighbor as myself.

Lord,
forgive me that I am inclined,
chiefly, to love myself.
Help me to hunger and thirst
for what is right,
to resist the temptation of those things
that are neither true nor honorable.
Help me to seek out
the things that are lovely.
Guide my thoughts
that I might think
the best of people,
and my words
that I might speak kindly
or not at all.

Feed my spirit
with wholesome food,
with generosity and loyalty.
Train my appetite to be satisfied
with nothing less than goodness.
Put love in my heart,
honesty in my mind,
truth on my lips,
and integrity in my bones.

6. THE MERCIFUL
(Matthew 5:7)

*Blessed are the merciful,
for they shall obtain mercy.*

Mercy is a large-hearted word.
It speaks of compassion,
unmerited forgiveness,
priceless generosity,
unearned, undeserved;
the gift of strength
put to service or laid aside
by kings, rulers, and judges.
And yet,
it is within my realm
to be merciful.

It is within my gift
to contribute from the well of mercy
that I drink from.
It is within my power,
lavishly or carefully,
to do something for the poor,
the hungry, and the naked of the world;

and were they on my doorstep
perhaps I would be moved to action.

The poor of the world
are on my doorstep,
but I cannot bear
to gaze upon their suffering.
There are those who need mercy,
comfort, and healing
who are only an arm's length
away from me;
in my street, amongst my friends,
in my family.

Lord,
fill me with compassion
for the hungry,
for the lonely,
for the sick, the dying,
and the bereaved.
As your mercy to me never ceases,
may that same mercy
be reflected in my life.

7. THE PURE IN HEART
(Matthew 5:8)

Blessed are the pure in heart,
for they shall see God.

Fragile purity suffers constant attack.
Grace, modesty, and chastity
are such easy prey
for hawkish derision.
Decency is dismissed as old-fashioned,
while simplicity and honesty
are merely the butts of sarcasm.

Yet the pure in heart survive
long after the last wounding arrow
has pierced this poor virtue,
for pure spirit cannot die.

How easily and often
evil slips my guard.
Deftly disguised,
he steps into conversations

with rakish ease
behind a smokescreen of flattery.
"It's a trifle risqué,
but you are a man of the world;
you're a broadminded chap;
can't shock you, can I?"
And then, perfumed foulness
defiles my ears,
and I smile
a traitorous smile.

Blessed are the pure in heart
for they shall see God.
And the pure in heart do see
virtue, goodness, and truth,
and that same loveliness
is seen in them.
It is written on their brows,
in their eyes,
and on their lips.

Lord,
when evil lays its snares,
when sophistication sneers at innocence,
write your truth indelibly
in my mind,
that my eyes might see
the power of purity.
Keep me, for Christ's sake,
pure in heart.

8. THE PEACEMAKERS
(Matthew 5:9)

Blessed are the peacemakers,
for they shall be called
the children of God.

How often people do evil
in the name of God.
How often has the name of God
been used as a cloak
for greed and aggression.
Even wars have been called *holy*.
The name of God has been desecrated
by oaths and curses,
called down as an excuse for violence.
People have laid the blame for their sins
on God's doorstep,
seemingly unaware
that the essence of God
is not retribution and anger,
but love.

Christ, the Prince of Peace,
said, "Love one another

as I have loved you."
"Turn the other cheek."
"Go the extra mile."
"Pray for those who persecute you."
"Love your enemies."

"You have heard it said,
'Thou shall not kill,'
but I say to you
that everyone who is angry with his brother
shall be liable to judgment."
The word of God is love,
his message is peace,
and the children of God
are peacemakers.

Lord,
when angry voices are raised,
may your peace be on my lips;
when evil is being thought and said,
may your gentle goodness be in my heart;
when jealousy or spite is abroad,
may your reconciling love be in my mind;
when injury or hurt is caused,
may your healing power be in my hands;
when dark injustice clouds the innocent,
may your wisdom light my path.

9. THEIRS IS THE KINGDOM
(Matthew 5:10)

Blessed are those who are persecuted
for righteousness' sake,
for theirs is the kingdom of heaven.

Lord,
I am afraid of persecution,
afraid of argument,
afraid of looking a fool,
afraid to stand and be counted a disciple.

It is not a real fear,
it is laziness.
It is less trouble
to be quiet, to say nothing;
less trouble
to be one of the crowd,
even when I know
that if the name of my God
and everything he stands for
is under attack,
my silence
is the loudest denial.

Lord,
you taught your first disciples
that they were the salt of the earth,
told them not to hide their light
under bushels,
but to show that light,
not only in words
but in their lives;
touch my tongue
with the salt of courage,
light my eyes
with the lamp of truth,
so that when righteousness
is persecuted,
I might, at whatever cost,
bear witness to the love
that opens the gates
of the kingdom of heaven.

10. LET THE LIGHT SHINE
(Matthew 5:16)

Let your light shine before others,
so that they may see your good works
and give glory to your Father in heaven.

It isn't easy
to do good quietly,
to be generous anonymously.
It isn't easy
to make secret sacrifices,
to do loving things
and not seek acknowledgment
or gratitude.
It isn't easy
to let my light illumine God,
to let goodness be glorified,
to let love be praised for its own sake.

Lord,
I confess that my love
is usually centered around myself;
that what good I do
is tarnished by my need

to be seen to be good.
Even my modesty
is a polished, self-conscious art.

Dear God,
show me
how to delight in love,
for love's sake;
how to be satifisfied with giving,
for its own sake;
how to make sacrifices,
for your sake;
how to let my light shine,
not on myself, but on you,
to whom I owe everything.
May those good works I am able to do
be seen for what they are—
reflections of your mercy,
your love, your glory.

11. LOVE YOUR ENEMIES
(Matthew 5:44)

Love your enemies.

Lord, you seem to be asking me
to fly in the face of nature.
When someone hurts me
I find I strike back
almost instantly,
an immediate reaction
that seems to be instinctive.
Hurt and resentment
are difficult springboards
for love.
Friends are sometimes
difficult to love,
and yet you ask that I should
love my enemies.

The nations of the world
appear committed
to instant retribution,
threat, and counter-threat.
The balance of power

seems to be a balance of fear.
It is popular belief that
"Only fools turn the other cheek,"
only fools—
and you Lord.
Only you intercede
for those who persecute you;
only you,
and those who possess your love,
love their enemies.

Before my enemies
and before my friends
I am the commander
of a host of things unlovely.
Deep within,
yet swift to emerge,
lie anger and suspicion.
In dark corridors
envy lurks with jealousy,
easily offended pride
sits on my shoulder,
and everything I do
that is selfish or unkind
is the enemy of love.

I am my own enemy.
I have even shaken my fist
at you,
and yet you love me.

Lord,
help me surrender
to your love,

that with your grace
I might learn
to turn the other cheek,
to walk the extra mile,
and to love my enemies,
for your sake.

12. OUR FATHER
(Matthew 6:9-10)

Our Father who art in heaven,
hallowed be thy name,
thy kingdom come,
thy will be done,
   on earth as it is in heaven.

As Jesus taught,
I dare to pray,
dare to call Almighty God
"Father,"
dare to hope for the love,
the patience, and the forgiveness
of a father,
dare to see myself
as a child of God.

"Who art in heaven."
The words conjure up a prospect to baffle poets.
Heaven, the dream beyond all dreams!
What horizons, skies, mountains, seas,
what birds sing,
in heaven?

What colors, what hills and streams
wait in the eternal refuge of the traveler?

What music, what laughter, what conversation
will fill an eternity of paradise?
What leaves tremble
over the resting place of courage?
What rendezvous are kept
at the meeting place of every face
that ever loved,
from the beginning to the end
of love itself?
Father,
hallowed be your name.

"Thy kingdom come,
thy will be done."
Some day,
envy, greed, and malice
will die of shame.
Some day,
the insanity of violence and war
will be healed.
Some day,
the sickness of sin
will be cured,
and the kingdom of love
will be revealed
on earth,
as it is in heaven.
Father,
may your kingdom come
and your will be done—
soon.

13. OUR DAILY BREAD
(Matthew 6:11)

Give us this day our daily bread.

With these words
I feel the guilt
of the rich man
who asks for more,
the guilt of knowing
I receive my daily bread
and enough to share.

"Give us this day
our daily bread."
Can I ask for daily bread
when a third of the world
is hungry?

Can I ask for daily bread
when the poor
live in hovels?
Can I ask for daily bread
when people
die on pavements?

Lord,
you have given us bread;
you have given us sufficient
and more—
and we have wallowed
in our wealth.

"Give us this day
our daily bread."
We have made
mountains of fruit and butter.
We have made
lakes of wine.
We have loaded ships
with surplus grain
and dumped it in the sea.
Like the feeding of the thousands
on the mountainside,
we could fill
the baskets of the world,
with the scraps left over.

Lord,
show me
how to share
my daily bread.

14. FORGIVE US
(Matthew 6:12)

Forgive us our trespasses.

What are my trespasses?
To *trespass* is to *exceed,*
to go beyond
what is honorable, just, or right.
To offend, to sin,
to inflict injury upon another,
is to trespass against God and Man.

I confess
I have trespassed against kindness,
I have offended gentleness and peace,
I have sinned in anger and selfishness,
I have inflicted injury on others
as much in the things I have chosen not to do
as in the things I have done.
The wounds of Christ bear witness
to every sin against justice and humanity.
Father,
forgive us our trespasses.

Father,
forgive me the petty sins
of a working day.
Forgive the curt remarks,
the mean self-interest
that misses opportunities
for caring, sharing, loving.

Lord,
as you do not bear grudges
against me,
let me not bear grudges
against anyone.
As you do not cling
to the memory of my sins,
let me forget
the wrongs I have suffered.

Father,
forgive us our trespasses,
as we forgive those
who trespass against us.

15. TESTING
(Matthew 6:13)

Lead us not into temptation.

Lord,
in my life temptations seem to abound,
seem to lie in wait
at every corner:
in conversation,
the temptation to speak evil of another;
in success,
the temptation to envy;
in every petty frustration and delay,
the temptation to anger.
Father,
let me not be tested
more than I can bear.

Father,
I am surrounded
by temptation to sin
in thought and in deed.

In my moments of weakness,
be my strength.

When I must decide,
guide me.
Let me choose
love and not hatred.
Let me choose
love and not anger.
Let me choose
love and not envy.
Let me choose
love and not evil.

Father,
do not let me be tested
beyond my endurance.
Do not put me on trial.
When I am tempted,
let me see your face.
When words form in my mind,
let me hear your voice.
When I am moved to action,
let me feel your hand on my arm.
May my thoughts, words, and deeds
be guided by your wisdom,
that temptation may lose its power
because of your presence.
Father,
lead us not into temptation.

16. TRIALS
(Matthew 6:13)

Deliver us from evil.

Men and women facing terrible trials
have cried out,
"Deliver us from evil."
That deliverance is always at hand,
in Jesus Christ,
the Lamb of God,
who bears the sins,
the fears, the pain and suffering
of the world, of all humankind.

When evil has so enslaved humans
that they inflict the worst
that one can do to another,
still, we are delivered
from death to life,
from dark to light,
to that world of light,
here and beyond,
where evil cannot survive.
Lord,
deliver me from evil.

Father,
open my eyes to all the places
where evil lurks.
Help me see through all the disguises
adopted by evil.
Let me see the evil
that hopes to ensnare
and capture my soul,
that I might do battle.
Let evil be exposed
wherever it hides,
wherever lies pretend to truth.

Lord,
deliver me from evil
in all its forms.

Father,
you are the love
that rescues me from evil;
you are the love
that saves me from danger;
you are the love
that frees me from captivity;
you are the love
that heals my suffering;
you are the love
that releases me from the prison of sin;
you are the love
that liberates me from the fear of death.
For your love has conquered
suffering, sin, and death.
Father,
in Christ's name,
deliver us from evil.

17. TREASURE
(Matthew 6:21)

*. . . where your treasure is,
there will you heart be also.*

It is easy to say
"My treasure lies
in those I love."
But do I treasure them
more than my favorite things,
more than status,
more than money,
more than self-esteem?
Does my world revolve
around those I love,
or do they revolve
around me
and the things I possess?

I would be dishonest
if I did not admit to wanting
earthly treasure.
I like being surrounded
by the things that give me pleasure

even when I can see how transitory,
how really worthless they are.
Lord,
let me *like* my *things,*
but let me *love* my *friends.*
In your mercy,
show me the true value of my own life.

Lord,
let me seek treasure
that time will not corrupt;
let me store up friendship;
let me collect laughter;
let me be rich in faith;
let me value hope;
let me covet the sparkling gems
of patience, kindness, gentleness,
large-heartedness, and understanding;
let me possess
the love that dies to self,
that I might gain the incorruptible treasure
of love that never dies.

18. ANXIETY
(Matthew 6:34)

Do not be anxious about tomorrow.

In circles and spirals
turning in my head,
I fear the things to come,
the words that might be said.
I fear disappointment,
failure, and blame;
I anticipate the worst,
I anticipate the shame.
While anxiety and worry,
the weapons of fear,
fight tomorrow's battles
before tomorrow's here.

It makes no sense
to borrow
the fretful possibilities
belonging to tomorrow.
Why have I failed to learn
what experience has taught:
that future ills

grow twice as large
when fed on present thought.

Time and time again,
when problems disappear,
I find I've been a hostage
to nothing more than fear.

Forgive my lack of faith, Lord,
my feeble loss of nerve,
my failing ability
to draw from your reserve
of strength and grace
and healing power,
my strong support
in every hour.

Lord,
let me walk
within your sight
and tomorrow's fears
are put to flight.

19. JUDGING
(Matthew 7:1)

Judge not, that you be not judged.

I never think of myself
as someone who judges others,
but I do, almost unconsciously.
I judge people I have never met
from secondhand stories.
I judge people
by their appearance,
by their conversation,
their mannerisms.
I pigeonhole people for years
because of a single incident.

Naturally,
I judge myself to be fair,
broadminded, generous,
reasonable, just.
I judge myself
as the person I imagine myself to be,
rather than the person I am.

Perhaps if I were more honest
with myself,
if I could really see myself as I am,
I might be kinder
in my judgments of others.

Lord,
who am I
to judge my fellows?
I can never know enough
to judge anyone.
In your presence we are all judged
and found wanting.
I am judged in ways I cannot measure
or imitate.
By goodness condemned,
by love restored,
by forgiveness healed,
I receive not justice,
but mercy.

Lord,
if it is human nature
to make judgments,
teach me to judge
as I am judged,
by you.

20. SOLID ROCK
(Matthew 7:24-27)

. . . like a wise man
who built his house on rock.

So much of my life
stands on uncertain ground,
on sands of doubt and fear,
in marshes of self-interest,
in the mud and clay
of money and possessions.
When the winds of ill-fortune,
pain, and bereavement
strike my house,
there is no strength
to endure the storm.

Yet in my distress
the hand of Christ
stretches out to lift me
across the threshold of his peace.
Through the mists of anxiety
there are glimpses of the mansions
prepared for me,

mansions built
on the rock of Christ's word.

Lord,
when everything about me
is uncertain,
may I remember your unshakable truth;
when I have been disappointed
by false friends,
may I put my trust in you;
when I face
unexpected intolerance,
may I turn to your unchanging mercy;
when I am rejected,
may I know your endless forgiveness.

Lord Jesus Christ,
you are the same
yesterday, today, and forever.
Help me build my life
on you,
so that when the winds blow
I will not be afraid,
but will stand firm in the knowledge
that your love can never fail,
and your word
is the rock that cannot move.

21. I AM NOT WORTHY
(Matthew 8:8-13)

Lord,
I am not worthy . . .
And Jesus said,
"Go, be it done for you
as you have believed."

Lord,
I am not worthy
to ask anything of you.
But you have continually
poured out your love
on the unworthy.
It is your nature to love
the helpless and the hopeless.
Neither is your love distant,
or a far-off dream.
You come to where the fallen lie.

Lord,
I am not worthy,
but I know
that I have only to ask

and I am at once
in your healing presence.

Lord,
I am not physically ill,
but I am weak
from lack of trust,
a surfeit of self,
and a deficiency of love.
My vision is restricted
because I fail to look up.
My world is reduced
because of a smallness of heart.

Lord,
I am not worthy.
Say but the word
and I shall be healed.

In your presence
I have no need to beg,
no need to explain.
To be in your presence
is to be made whole.

Lord,
give me my mustard seed of faith
that will move a mountain of fears,
that will overcome anxieties and uncertainties
and enable me to live
the life I was intended to live.
Give me
the faith that will tune my ears
to hear you say,
"Go, what you believe will be done."

22. WHY ARE YOU AFRAID?
(Matthew 8:24-26)

And behold,
there arose a great storm on the sea,
so that the boat was being swamped
by the waves;
but he was asleep.
And they went and woke him, saying,
"Save, Lord, we are perishing."
And he said to them,
"Why are you afraid, O men of little faith?"
Then he rose
and rebuked the winds and the sea;
and there was a great calm.

From a fierce wind
and a white-capped sea,
I've stepped inside a chartroom,
closed the door and been shocked
by the calm of that inner refuge.
Not that the storm had died,
for the wind still raged
beyond the door,
waiting.

"Why are you afraid, O men of little faith?"
I have been afraid—so many times;
afraid of injury or illness,
afraid of being alone,
afraid of people.
I have been afraid of love,
afraid that it might overwhelm me like the sea.
I have been afraid of truth,
because it threatened to change my life.
I have been afraid of the future,
afraid of uncharted waters,
afraid until I pray,
"Lord, save me or I perish,"
and entering his presence
there is a great calm.

"Why are you afraid, O men of little faith?
for I am with you in the storm,
with you in fear,
with you in noise,
with you in quiet,
with you in laughter,
with you in suffering,
with you in death,
with you in paradise."

Lord,
build up my little faith
to know and trust
that in your presence,
there is a great calm.

23. HEALING
(Matthew 9:12-13)

Jesus said,
"Those who are well
have no need of a physician,
but those who are sick.
Go and learn what this means,
'I desire mercy, and not sacrifice.'
For I came not to call the righteous,
but sinners."

And it is easy to *say,*
"That's me, a sinner,"
but who would call himself
righteous?
In politics, in war,
in private life,
I am always "on the side of right."
My arguments are rational.
My actions are justifiable.
My decisions are dictated by conscience.
I do my best to be a "good chap."
So how could I be sick?
Or a sinner in need of mercy?

I call myself a sinner,
but do I really believe it?
Pride even convinces me
that I possess humility.

Lord,
pride and sin
nailed love upon a cross.
May that love
persuade me of my need
for forgiveness.
May that love,
and only that love,
inform my arguments,
justify my actions.
May that love
be my conscience.
May that love
enable me to come to you
for healing,
O physician of my soul.

24. SPEAKING OUT
(Matthew 10:19-20)

Do not be anxious ... what you are to say;
for what you are to say will be given you
in that hour;
for it is not you who speak,
but the Spirit of your Father speaking through you.

I have so often thought,
"If only I had the right words.
If only I was clever enough."
In a moment of crisis
I am feeble, afraid to speak.
It is not merely a failure of nerve,
but rather a failure of faith.

Lord,
I am not brave.
I am not the stuff
that martyrs are made of.
I would rather not hear, not see.
I would rather turn away.
I would like an undisturbed life,

but there is no escape
for I cannot love you and be totally silent.

Lord,
let me trust in your promise
that in dark times
I will not be alone.
Help me realize
that your Holy Spirit
will come to my rescue,
will provide the words.
Give me faith to rely on you,
to believe that you will hear my cry.

I have no strength
but your strength;
no wisdom
but your wisdom;
no words worth hearing,
unless you speak.
Lord,
in that hour
be in my heart and on my lips.

25. REAL LIFE
(Matthew 10:39)

Those who find their life will lose it.

It is such a difficult idea,
to die to yourself in order to live.
I am at the center of my world.
The world revolves around me,
my needs, my desires,
my ambitions, my will.
How can I die to myself?

I die to myself
when I am loving.
Love is forgetful of self,
is self-sacrificing,
is self-denying.
The heartbeat of real life
is love.
Love is reality,
it is the spirit of God
in all of us.

There is an illusion
that deceives from time to time,
the thought that a better life would be possible
if I were surrounded by better things.
But the illusion is deadly,
for devotion to things
is soul-destroying.
Possessions enslave.
Captured by self-interest, self-concern,
I am loveless and lifeless.
There is no room for the spirit of love,
there is no time to live.

Lord,
when I am drowsy
with the drug of self,
wake me, lead me on;
when I am imprisoned
by the things of this world,
may your spirit release me;
when I am more concerned with myself
than with those I have been given to love,
save me from myself,
that I might live to explore
the heart of love,
where riches and wealth
are measured by truth and compassion,
where the journey never ends
but endlessly delights,
where being lost in love,
the treasure of life is found.

26. REST
(Matthew 11:28-30)

*"Come to me, all who labor
and are heavy laden
and I will give you rest.
Take my yoke upon you,
and learn from me;
for I am gentle and lowly in heart,
and you will find rest for your souls.
For my yoke is easy,
and my burden is light."*

From time to time
I am laden
with anxiety,
anxiety that weighs heavily
and depresses;
fear
that brings me to my knees;
bereavement
that leaves me weak and helpless.
My yoke is heavy
with lies and betrayal,

greed and selfishness,
pain and disappointment.

Lord,
I lay my burdens at your feet
and I ask for rest.
The weight of my burdens
is known to you,
for you carried them
on the cross.
The burden of my sin and failure
was lifted, balanced,
and outweighed by love.

Lord,
put your yoke
upon my shoulders
that I may know
the burden of love
is light.

Lord,
my labor is heavy with pride
and slow to forgive.
I am burdened with laziness,
with lack of concern
for the poor, the hungry, and the sick.

Lord,
forgive me;
weigh me down with your love
that my burden may be light.

27. WHITED SEPULCHRES
(Matthew 15:10-20; 23:27)

And he said to them:
"It is not what goes into the mouth
that defiles a person,
but what comes out of the mouth.
For out of the heart come evil thoughts,
murder, adultery, fornication,
theft, false witness, slander.
These are what defile a person."
And again, he said:
"Woe unto you, scribes and Pharisees,
hypocrites!
for you are like whitewashed tombs
which outwardly appear beautiful,
but within they are
full of the bones of the dead
and all uncleanness."

No wonder they sought to destroy him.
Who can bear to be called a hypocrite?
Clean on the outside and rotten within.
Yet here I stand, alongside the Pharisee,
no less guilty of paying homage

to outward appearances.
Outwardly I hope to appear
generous, kind, and caring,
when deep within lies
selfishness, meanness, envy, and anger.

Lord,
forgive me
that I try to whitewash my failings,
that I try to cover up,
rather than condemn,
everything that is unlovely within me.
Let me not playact at being your disciple.
Fill my heart with your spirit,
that the thoughts of my mind
and the words of my lips
may be your thoughts,
your words,
your love.

28. WHO DO YOU SAY THAT I AM?
(Matthew 16:13-16)

*Now when Jesus came
into the district of Caesarea Philippi,
he asked his disciples,
"Who do people say the Son of man is?"
And they said,
"Some say John the Baptist,
and others say Elijah,
and others Jeremiah, or one of the prophets."
He said to them,
"But who do you say that I am?"
Simon Peter replied,
"You are the Christ,
the Son of the living God."*

Christ's question
echoes from generation to generation,
a disturbing, personal question,
"But who do *you* say that I am?"
Not the question of a wise man or prophet,
not, "What do you think of my words?"
nor, "Do you understand my teaching?"
but, "Who do you say that I am?"

The mystery of Christ
lies not in what he said or taught
but in who he was.

And who do I say he is?
I say the name, Jesus Christ,
and I see eyes of unlimited compassion,
I see hands that heal,
I hear the voice of forgiveness and truth,
I feel the love that conquers pain,
I see, hear, and feel
the presence of God.

Sin is judged
by goodness, love, and truth.
Unable to face this judgment
goodness is derided,
truth is twisted,
and love is crucified.

Lord,
help me climb the hill of truth,
walk the path of goodness,
live the life of love.
Help me declare, with some part of my life,
that you are the Christ,
the Son of the living God.

29. LIKE CHILDREN
(Matthew 18:3)

*Truly I say to you, unless you turn
and become like children,
you will never enter
the kingdom of heaven.*

But how can I become like a child?
In what way?
What have I lost since childhood?
Humility, obedience, innocence?
Surely, innocence lost
cannot be regained?

Lord,
I can no longer see
with eyes of a child.
I have been taught
to be independent,
to be self-assured.

Innocence has become mere naïveté
and my worldly wisdom
has made heaven distant.

So what must I do
to enter the kingdom?
How can I become like a child?

In children
I see unself-conscious joy,
receptive faces,
total dependence.
And there's the difference.
Children do not earn love
or achieve happiness.
They simply accept what is given them.
To a child
the gates of heaven are not conquered
by knowledge,
or forced by superhuman effort;
they open—by grace.

Lord,
help me accept
like a child
the love I have not earned,
that I might enjoy
the peace that passes understanding.

30. SEVENTY TIMES SEVEN
(Matthew 18:21-22)

*Then Peter said to him,
"Lord, how often shall my brother
sin against me, and I forgive him?
As many as seven times?"
Jesus said to him,
"I do not say to you seven times,
but seventy times seven."*

Lord,
you have forgiven me
so often;
teach me to forgive.
It is somehow
easier to judge
than to forgive;
to point the finger,
to shake the head,
even when I know
that I look down on others
from the height of my own folly,
from a judgment seat
insecurely perched

on the self-made mountain
of my own mistakes.
For the sins I condemn the most
are those that echo mine.

Lord,
teach me to forgive,
to recognize myself
in the human frailty of others.
I need forgiveness
every hour of every day,
forgiveness for my thoughts,
forgiveness for my words,
forgiveness for my deeds.
Lord,
through your love
I am forgiven.
Through your grace
may I be forgiving.

31. THE RESURRECTION OF THE DEAD
(Matthew 22:31-33)

*And Jesus said,
"As for the resurrection of the dead,
have you not read
what was said to you by God,
'I am the God of Abraham,
the God of Isaac,
and the God of Jacob'?
He is not the God of the dead,
but of the living."
And when the crowd heard it,
they were astonished at his teaching.*

And still,
life after death is doubted.
Heaven is seen by some
as a comforting dream
invented for the bereaved.

And still,
the people are astonished
at his teaching.
But Christ did not only teach,
he declared truth

and lived it.
He preached love
and showed it.
He promised resurrection,
and his wounded feet
walked to Emmaus,
and his pierced hands
broke bread.

Lord,
you promised to prepare
a place for us,
for me,
in your father's house,
a promise underlined
by the words,
"If it were not so,
I would have told you."
My Lord and my God,
a heavenly reunion
outside the bounds of time
is too great a vision
for my mind to encompass.

But I know
that love cannot die,
truth cannot die—
and you are
perfect love
and perfect truth.

Lord,
with all my limitations,
I believe;
help my unbelief.

32. THE GREAT COMMANDMENT
(Matthew 22:36-40)

"Teacher,
which is the great commandment
in the law?"
And he said to him,
"You shall love the Lord your God
with all your heart,
and with all your soul,
and with all your mind.
This is the great and first commandment.
And the second is like it,
You shall love your neighbor
as yourself.
On these two commandments
depend all the law and prophets."

Dear Lord,
the great commandments are so clear,
so direct—
and so difficult.

Loving my neighbor
somehow seems less complex

than loving God.
To do a good turn for a friend,
to be helpful to a neighbor,
to befriend a stranger:
these things are so easy to substitute
for loving God.
Yet the first and great commandment
is not to love my neighbor,
but to love the Lord my God
with all my heart,
with all my soul,
and with all my mind.

Love is devoted,
love cares,
love listens and watches and learns.
Love lavishes time on the beloved.
So, help me, Lord,
to listen and watch that I might learn of you.
Help me to surrender my time to you
that I might be aware of you
from my waking to my sleeping.

Let me hold open
the doors to my heart and mind
that your love might enter
every part of my being,
that through my hands,
through my voice,
through my life,
my neighbors may know
your love.

33. THE LEAST OF THESE
(Matthew 25:37-40)

Then the righteous will answer him,
"Lord, when did we see you hungry and feed you,
or thirsty, and give you drink?
And when did we see you a stranger and welcome you,
or naked and clothe you?
And when did we see you sick
or in prison and visit you?"
And the King will answer them,
"Truly, I say to you,
as you did it to one
of the least of these my brethren,
you did it to me."

Lord,
you came to reveal your love
to the poor and the sick,
the outcast and the sinner.
You shared, you healed,
you embraced, you forgave;
and wherever there is poverty,
sickness, or anguish,

you are there in the midst.
In hospitals, in prisons,
in barren places and battlefields
and in cities,
your voice cries out,
"Father, I thirst."

Wherever people are oppressed
by tyrants,
tyrants with armies
or tyrants in factories,
offices, or homes,
you are there.
Wherever your children suffer
you weep with them.
Wherever there is deprivation
it is you who are deprived.

Lord,
may I find some way
to ease some of the suffering,
some way to offer
food and water,
comfort and aid,
to some of your children in need.
When the suffering look at me,
may I see your eyes.
When the poor ask for comfort,
may I see your face.
When the hungry cry out,
may I hear your voice,
so that one day
I may hear you say,
"As you did it to one of these,
you did it unto me."

34. TAKE, EAT
(Matthew 26:26-29)

*Now as they were eating,
Jesus took bread, and blessed, and broke it,
and gave it to the disciples and said,
"Take, eat; this is my body."
And he took a cup,
and when he had given thanks
he gave it to them, saying,
"Drink of it, all of you;
for this is my blood of the covenant,
which is poured out for many
for the forgiveness of sins.
I tell you I shall not drink again
of this fruit of the vine
until that day when I drink it new
with you in my Father's kingdom."*

In chapels and churches,
in villages, towns, and cities,
in cathedrals and convents,
in hospitals and homes,
from sunrise to sunset,
these words of Christ are spoken,

"Take, eat; this is my body."
And the life that was laid down
lives and breathes in every soul
that comes to his table.
The miracle and the mystery
of the resurrected Christ
is not theory or theological surmise,
but a living fact,
when the source of love takes residence
in the hearts of those who love him.

Dear Lord,
this body,
this blood,
this bread,
this wine,
this lover's tryst with you
is the living heart of faith.
From this communion
comes love and hope.
From this communion
comes forgiveness and peace.
From this communion
comes healing and strength.
From this communion
comes life that never ends.

Lord,
may I live in communion with you,
now and always.

35. BEFORE THE COCK CROWS
(Matthew 26:34)

Jesus said to him,
"Truly I say to you,
this very night,
before the cock crows,
you will deny me three times."

Peter,
so like all of us;
wanting to be heroic,
to be brave, to be good,
to be loved,
yet failing.
When I think of my own good intentions,
I see resolutions that came to nothing
and promises broken.
How many times have I determined
to turn over a new leaf
only to discover
that I am not as strong as I thought,
not as generous,
not as fearless,
not as loving.

For me, Peter,
the cock crows almost every day.

Lord,
when I have denied you
through selfishness,
when I have chosen
to stand alongside those
who persecute you,
I have cried,
"I do not know the man."

Lord,
when I have allowed
anger to rule rather than forgiveness,
when I have thought or spoken
ill of another,
my words have declared,
"I do not know the man."

Lord,
when I have denied the truth,
when I have deceived;
kept silent in the face of lies,
my silences have shouted,
"I do not know the man."

Lord,
forgive me.
Strengthen my resolve;
help me grow in goodness;
let me hear you ask,
"Do you love me?"
before the cock crows.

36. TAKE THIS CUP
(Matthew 26:39)

And going a little further
he fell on his face and prayed,
"My Father,
if it be possible,
let this cup pass from me;
nevertheless, not as I will,
but as thou wilt."

Lord,
how many times have I cried,
"Take this cup from me."
How often have I prayed,
"Save me from what lies ahead,"
only to feel
that my words were echoing
in deep silence?

But the silence of the deaf
and the silence of the listening
are entirely different.

Father,
you could not have been deaf
to the cries from Gethsemane;
nor blind
to that staggering climb on Calvary;
nor unmoved
by the words, "I thirst."
How terrifying
is the silence of your listening!

The silence of my God
is filled with power,
the power of love
so concentrated,
so intense,
so razor-sharp
that sin and death are severed,
and neither knows
it is no longer relevant.

The power of resurrecting
Easter love pierces history
and explodes in glory beyond time
with such brilliance
that the heavens applaud
in awestruck silence.

And in that silence,
my cry, my ache, my sorrow
are taken from me,
and every pain ever felt
is engulfed by love—
endless, eternal, infinite love.
Father,
not my will,
but your will be done.

37. THE SPIRIT IS WILLING
(Matthew 26:41)

Watch and pray
that you may not enter into temptation;
the spirit indeed is willing,
but the flesh is weak.

It seems as if the whole of life
is a battle
between the spirit and the flesh,
between what is temporary and passing
and what is eternal,
between reality and unreality.
Few of us are visionaries.
Most of us live with immediate things.
The things we can see and touch seem real
and we cling to them for security.
Yet they are the very things
which, in time, will cease to be.
The only thing that is eternal is the spirit.
Yet my flesh continues
its battle against the spirit.

My spirit is courageous,
but I play it safe.
My spirit is generous,
but I count the pennies.
My spirit is self-sacrificing,
but I'm too tired.

My spirit is gentle,
but my mouth is hard.
My spirit believes,
but my ears doubt.
My spirit is warm,
but my eyes are cold.
My spirit is willing,
but my flesh is weak.

Lord,
unite my spirit with yours
so that selfishness, greed,
envy, anger, and idleness—
all that is unworthy and unloving,
all that defiles and contradicts my spirit,
all that prevents me from reaching
the stature that was intended for me—
may be overcome by your never-ending love,
and I might watch,
not one hour but eternity
with you.

38. LOVE IS CRUCIFIED
(Matthew 27:46)

My God, my God,
why hast thou forsaken me?

That terrible, painful, plaintive cry,
from the brink of hell
rings through time and beyond.
For Christ died
beneath the weight
of all the lovelessness and sin
that ever was
or is to be.

Love is crucified every single day,
nailed to a cross of wood;
love is made to pay.
Every cruel thought, a thorn in his head,
nailed to a cross of wood,
love lies dead.

Love is crucified for love of me,
nailed to a cross of wood,
hung on a tree.

All my evil deeds pierce through his side;
nailed to a cross of wood,
Jesus died.

Love is cruicifed by mortar and by shell;
nailed to a cross of wood,
love meets hell.
Love is crucified below and above;
nailed to a cross of wood,
Christ is love.

Risen Lord,
forgive me for my part in your passion.
Forgive me that my sins
are taunts from the foot of the cross.
Forgive me for my part
in the suffering of the world,
that I do so little
to meet the needs of others.

Father,
forgive them
who do not know what they do;
and although I cannot claim
innocence or ignorance,
Father,
in your mercy,
forgive me.

(The song "Love Is Crucified" is from the author's radio play, *On the Hill.*)

39. TO THE END OF THE WORLD
(Matthew 28:20)

Lo, I am with you always,
to the close of the age.

How bleak
that sad, dead day
the tomb was sealed with stone.
How deep the groans of grief
from those who had talked
and laughed and ate
and shared the dusty road;
had seen the eyes,
had touched the hands,
had heard the voice
that promised life.

And then,
mourners on the road to Emmaus
broke bread and saw his face.
At a breakfast meal
on a fisherman's beach,
his broken hands gave bread,
and those who witnessed knew

that the Lord of love
crucified and buried,
was the Lord of life.

Risen Lord,
who, every day, triumphs over death,
you are with us now.
Let me live my life
aware of your presence.
Open my eyes that I might see
your thorn-crowned head
among the poor, the hungry,
the suffering and oppressed.
Make my heart your home
that from the deadness of sin
I might be raised to the life of love.

40. PEACE
(John 14:27)

Peace I leave with you;
my peace I give to you.

Peace seems to be so elusive,
fleeting, temporary,
like a rainbow that disappears
before I can enjoy it.
And when Jesus said,
"My peace I give to you,"
he was but hours away
from violence,
and death on a cross.
So where, and what
is his peace?

Before he went to the cross
Jesus said,
"Yet a little while
and the world will see me no more;
but you will see me.
Because I live,
you will live also."

His peace
comes from trust in him—
in his promise
that whatever we may face,
love can never be defeated.
"In the world you have tribulation,
but be of good cheer,
I have overcome the world."

May God grant us
peace from war, from civil strife,
peace of mind,
and a share of peace and quiet.
But most of all, may we know
his peace,
which is
the eye of the hurricane,
the calm
in the center of the storm,
the sure stillness
of love that never fails.
So may the peace of God,
which passes all understanding,
keep our hearts and minds
in the knowledge
and love of Christ.